THE THIRD VOICE

Fables in collaboration by two poets

Grace Cavalieri & Geoffrey Himes

BLUE LIGHT PRESS ❖ 1ST WORLD PUBLISHING

1ST WORLD
PUBLISHING

SAN FRANCISCO ❖ FAIRFIELD ❖ DELHI

The Third Voice

Copyright ©2025 by Grace Cavalieri & Geoffrey Himes

1st World Library
PO Box 2211
Fairfield, IA 52556
www.1stworldpublishing.com

Blue Light Press
www.bluelightpress.com
bluelightpress@aol.com

Book & Cover Design
Melanie Gendron
melaniegendron999@gmail.com

Cover Art
"Freedom" by Grace Cavalieri,
acrylic and wood putty

First Edition

Library of Congress Cataloging-in-Publication Data

ISBN: 978-1-4218-3581-5

Dedicated to our children

Table of Contents

Foreword

Art has many aims, but one of its primary goals is empathy. If a movie, symphony or poem can put us in another person's skin and make us see what that person sees, feel what that person feels, our consciousness is expanded, perhaps changed. Once we empathize with others, it's difficult to denigrate or dismiss them.

Such empathy can be achieved by the content of a novel or painting, but it can also be sparked by the process of creation. When two or more artists collaborate, they have to share two distinct perspectives to work effectively – and that inevitably alters the final product. Such collaboration is common in film, theater and popular song but rare in fiction and poetry.

For this book, *The Third Voice*, and its predecessor, *Fables from Italy and Beyond*, Grace Cavalieri and I co-wrote every poem. We each contributed lines of our own, rewrote the lines of the other and shuffled words until it was hard to remember who contributed what. We soon realized that these poems didn't sound like the poems she wrote on her own or those I wrote on my own. We had evolved a new voice, a third voice.

Having made the leap into each other's head, it was easier to put ourselves in the skin of the astronomers, flood victims, hitchhikers, tree frogs, monkeys, black birds, dying men, ventriloquist dummies and bank robbers who populate these poems. And from there into the imaginations of our readers.

– Geoffrey Himes

Astronomy

I asked the astronomer if
the observatory was open on Christmas.
Of course, he said. *The stars never sleep.*

I was awake all night,
aware of all those stars,
sleep-deprived, jittery.

I asked the astronomer if
I would ever sleep again.
Of course," he said. "*Your body will insist on it.*

But each eye in the sky
burns its way into my brain,
setting my every doubt on fire.

I asked the astronomer if
New Year's Day would bring relief.
Of course, he said. *One can get used to anything.*

Barroom Dancing

The ballet dancer wraps her thin branches
around the burly cowboy's oaken trunk.

He gulps down a whiskey.
She sips a veggie smoothie.

She clings tight and whispers *Giddyup* in his ear,
and he does. But she never loses her grip.

A bucking, kicking rodeo stallion,
he mounts the bar, her feathered arms round his neck.

Soon they are two spinning quarters on the bar top,
her tutu flouncing in the saddle.

As she hums the theme from "Swan Lake," he leaps
from table to table and breaks twenty-two chairs.

Stallion and swan spin out the swinging doors
into the cornfield across the street,

dancing horizontal between green stalks
as the moon kept the music going.

They say he grew lithe as a violin string
and she as boxy as a cello.

Parents tell this story as a warning
about dating outside your algorithm.

The Legend of Lancaster County

All the witnesses agreed.
The bank robber had two heads.
One head said, *Give me all your money.*
The other head said, *No, please don't.*

Harry, the left head, controlled the right side.
Donny, the right head, controlled the left.
Each head claimed innocence.
Each head blamed the other.

The cops called it a crime.
The lawyers called it a family feud.
The wife the brothers shared
could not testify against either one.

Her name was Mathilda,
ashamed she only had one head.
How much easier it would be
if she had a head for each brother.

The brothers argued, and she wept.
This went on for years.
The operation to give her a second head
would cost eighty thousand dollars.

We could rob a bank, said Harry,
but it would be wrong.
No, said Donny, *it would be right.*
Please don't do it, pleaded Mathilda.

Donny wore a lion mask.
Harry wore a horse mask.

Mathilda wore cold cream
and watched the evening news.

They were counting the money
when the cops burst in.
Not hard to find a two-headed
bank robber in Lancaster County.

Now it is visiting hour at the prison.
Mathilda looks at Donny's head, at Harry's head.
She looks at the reflection of her one
head in the plexiglass window.

Rice

She needed to see
her two ex-husbands side by side,
so she invited them both for dinner.

They each arrive expecting rekindled love
or at least filet mignon.
She serves them red beans and rice.

The first one says, *I see you remember
our honeymoon in New Orleans.
Mardi Gras is coming up.*

The second one says,
*I see you're not eating meat.
I'm thinking of becoming a vegetarian.*

The first interrupts the second.
The second interrupts the first.
She sits back, watches and listens.

Like rice in the pot on the stove,
her heart soaks up
the liquid it swims in.

Too much starch.
Not enough pepper.
Time to start over from scratch.

Her mama once told her,
*The secret to a good rice dish
is the right broth.*

The Lost Chord

A chord dazzled through the galaxy
and fell on farmers in the field.

Not everyone could hear it,
but the cows looked up in wonder.

The old men in their overalls
spun into dust devils in their waders.

No outsiders believed it,
but the locals swore on the Bible it was true.

They said butterflies large as floating hands
spiraled down within the sound.

They said daisies with blinking eyes
stretched their stems toward the sky.

Scientists snickered; reporters rolled their eyes,
but the witnesses would not change their story.

Dead tractors had come to life.
Barren fields had turned fertile.

The song that nested in their heads
had never been heard on any radio.

As for me, I play it furtively, in a locked room,
late at night, when no one else can hear.

Perilous Times

What do I have to do to be safe?
I calibrate my steps to never land on a crack.
The ground is strong, and the fall is deep.
Crows dive for your hair, so lift up your collar.

Forget architecture.
Plan for obsolescence.
The refrigerator is empty.
I have reservations at seven.

Are these bells of justice or of alarm?
First the city burns, then the county, then the country.
And this is the day my car got stolen,
all because I parked in the wrong place

The guard dog is snoring.
I forget who to call
when I lose my password.
If only I had a calendar.

Why sun in the evening, moon in the morning?
A computer that can defeat us at Go.
A baby bird grateful for a regurgitated worm.
This is episode one in a series of ten.

We had no place to play,
but that's the way the plant grows.
Once I thought the world was real,
and it was just a matter of bad air.

Where is the plan now that we need one?
Abandoned manuscripts stuffed in the wall for insulation,

tiny rear-view mirrors on my glasses.
I'm scraping the black paint from the windows.

We link arms at the elbows.
I can't save anyone but myself.
Youth is wasted on the young.
Death is wasted on the dead.

If this is the end, where do we go next?
The clearing in the woods is covered in moss.
I sift the ashes and my wedding ring appears.
I climb the stairs to her last known address.

The Tree Frog

The tree was wounded
where lightning
had struck a branch.
Worms and woodpeckers
created a hole
just large enough
for an orange tree frog
to emerge
glowing like a lantern.

I held it in my hand,
its long purple toes
tracing the broken lines
in my palm.

What am I to the forest
and the forest to me?
Roots and branches
reach into me and out from me
through words and birds.

Slimy as spilled juice, his freckled back
is sweating poisons. His bulging eyeball
tracks the sleeve of my orange parka
to the collar and my foreign face.

Down the twin spiraling staircases of DNA,
one step is shared by me and this frog.
It might be a link of fear.
It might be a bond of affection.

The frog leaps from my hand
into the hole in the tree,
stares back with bottomless black eyes,
beckons me to follow.

Lifted and Tilted

Lifted and tilted,
the house had been floating
down the river.
Now stranded by a sandbar,
white water for flooring,
granite cliffs for windows.

But on the second floor
a family eats its Christmas dinner
beneath a chandelier decked with holly.

Do they defy catastrophe
or ignore it?

The water rises; the water falls.
The house without its pillars
rides the tide
till stopped by a mountain.

A woman pulls a goose from the oven.
Her daughter pours pear cider in every glass.
Her son throws an oak log on the fire.
Her husband recites his grandfather's poem.

The house sheds shingles like October leaves.
A mandolin is heard from within.

Tintinabulation

I can hear bells singing
from someone else's childhood.
They sound farther away
the closer I get.

Nothing between
my head and my toes,
just a listening.

I walk under the mountain,
along the lake,
over the hill
to an abandoned church.

In the choir loft,
I find a traveling theater troupe
sleeping in piles of laundry.
In the sanctuary,
actors are stretching their legs
and goldening their vowels.
They ask me to play the part
of the grouchy elder
with a bell for a heart.

My feet are dancing.
My doors are opening.
My bell is ringing
from the church
over the hill
along the lake,
under the mountain.

Gold

If we never got what we wanted, we will never get what we seek.
I caught the rainbow by its tail and pulled it from its hole.
I tried to stroke and coax her to show me the hidden gold,
but it clawed and squealed like a cat in a half-filled bathtub.
We will never get the thing we want, if it refuses to be wanted.
The striped cat separated into seven different snakes with seven
different tails.
I greedily grabbed them like leashes, got pulled underground. The
unstoppable desire meets the unyielding object.
I followed the serpents into the blackened coal and found jewels,
red, orange, yellow, green, blue, indigo and violet.
But finding is easier than holding, holding harder than keeping.
I pocketed what I could grasp and rocketed to Utah.
Customs charged me with the seven cardinal sins.
I was sent to the salt flats; I crawled across the desert.
The hunt for treasure becomes the search for salvation.
Arroyos held only the memory of water, but cacti were in blossom.
Dusted with pollen and rusted with iron,
I crossed the sandstone arch of a fading rainbow.

Marriage Advice

I bought him a suit that was too small.
He bought me a hat I thought too large.

He took me to a beach that was too hot.
In my mountain cabin, he was too cold.

I ordered curry. He said, *Too spicy.*
He brought me sherbet. I thought, *Too icy.*

Because he loves me, he shivers on a mountain,
red-faced from curry in a jacket too tight.

And I lie beside him on the sand,
buns-in-the-sun, chewing ice in a lopsided hat.

Thanks for the Ride

A car pulls over to offer a ride.
The hitchhiker gets in and drives away.

Behind him, a bus turns northward
beneath the trees' green cathedral.

Trucks are turning left on Market Street.
An airplane is flying south overhead.

Baseballs and mitts smack the evening with leather.
Pot roast rubs the air with carrots and gravy.

Parking cars fill the driveways.
Flicked-on lights yellow the windows.

Behind him is his voice, high as a jay's,
and his father's, low as a crow's,

climbing the ladder of anger.
A woman weeps. A door slams.

Now he sits in a stranger's car,
his knapsack nestled in his lap.

Two books and a jar of peanut butter.
Four orange T-shirts, three pairs of socks.

Night Shift

She's spinning on the stool at the diner counter,
naked thighs beneath her swimsuit stuck to vinyl.
He's flipping hot cakes on the grill's sizzling grease.
He translates the order, *Adam and Eve on a raft*,
into two poached eggs on toast.

When his evening shift finally ends,
she wakes him with a steaming cup of joe.
Theirs is a 24 HOURS love like the window's
pink letters shining on the formica table.
They believe their hearts will NEVER CLOSE
like the flashing letters in neon blue.

They're holding hands between fries and burgers.
The parking lot empties and refills.
One waitress goes home and another comes on duty.
More slices of pie, apple-raisin and sour-cherry.
Red lipstick on the mug and on his neck.
Coins spilled across syrup-stained placemats.
The whole world narrowed to a single corner booth.

Planet of the Apes

Her pet monkey was missing,
not on his blanket, not on his swing.
She called out his name,
Lucky! but it came out, *Yuhwee!*
Her false teeth were missing too.
The water glass where she
kept them overnight was empty.
She reached for her pink bathrobe,
but the gold closet hook was bare.
She looked down for her fuzzy slippers,
but they were gone as well.

Shivering, barefoot in a thin nightgown,
she shuffled down the hall.
At the breakfast table was the monkey,
wearing her bathrobe, drinking her coffee,
smoking her cigarettes, reading her paper,
a fuzzy slipper dangling from his right foot,
and smiling a smile larger than his mouth.
The teeth needed brushing, the bathrobe mending.
He was too young to be smoking,
and he'd already done the puzzle.

Just Another Whistle Stop

It is our nature to wander.
Now we think we are lost.
We boarded a train with no schedule, no answer.
We disembarked at a meadow of blue flowers.
We put on overshoes to walk through
purple waves and golden corn.

The moon sets and the night begins
with a total eclipse of the sun.
Fireflies are stabbing the dark.
We can't see the persimmon tree,
but we can hear it moving.
We can't see the silver river,
but we can feel it cutting our throats.

My bloody voice cries out,
Our friends are all dying.
Consciousness bleeds from my neck,
and I fall asleep in the pasture
between two ticking bombs.

I wake in a treetop to nothing
but sky and water, water and sky,
circling sharks and vultures,
eaglets babbling in a nearby nest,
persimmons masquerading as tomatoes,
a train ticket tucked among the seeds.

I should have prepared some poems before I left home:
a poem of how to die successfully,
a poem of how to thread the maze between head and heart,
a poem of how to plant a tree that will attract the first deer I ever saw.

Trap Door

I didn't believe in magic, certainly not
from a rusty car outgrown by grass,
not until I crawled through the cabin window,

tripped over a toppled chair,
and somersaulted over a bucket,
onto the hardwood floor.

Staring up at peeling wallpaper,
frayed curtains were blowing over
a torn calendar. 1973.

I had been here before
at a party of city poets
out in the piney woods.

My cell phone dropped,
lighting up the ghosts
like a rocket.

They were hollow shells,
translucent and pearl-white,
making a low hum I couldn't decipher.

Ellen Carter, John Duchac, Bernard Welt,
Devy Bendit, Marty Brown, Paul Bartlett,
Gail Saunders, Alan Britt, Terence Winch.

Fifty years younger,
as I will always remember them,
flickering like half-engaged light bulbs.

Envy, lust and ambition hung in the air
like kitchen trash burning
in a backyard fire.

But when the smoke settled
and the flames sank into embers,
what remained was

thrilling language,
stolen kisses,
lingering affection.

Sudden Departure

I'm sorry I left your poetry reading early.
The poems were good, but it was unavoidable.
The car was on fire and the children were dying.
The cat was having kittens,
and the ice cream was melting.

I went out to look for you, but where your car had been,
all I found was a pumpkin and six white mice.
On the handicap ramp to the arts center, though,
I found a glass slipper that might be your size.

I'm sorry I left your poetry reading early.
Please don't look for something that can't be found.
The horse has left the barn.
The train has left the station.
Corn stalks in the field were turning brown
The crows were eating the scarecrow.

The slipper is in my bookbag as I'm banging on your door.
I know you're up there painting murals on the tower walls.
If you won't answer your phone, please let down your hair.

The Raven and the Crow

1
The crow noses through the high grass,
hunting the hiding field mouse.

The raven glides overhead, watching
for the slightest stirring of the stalks.

What keeps them moving, always moving?
Hunger, yes, but also something else.

2
Oh, raven, where do you fly so far?
What grows on the trees beyond the mountain?

Oh, crow, where do you hide in the forest?
What rare animals live in the briars?

Oh, black birds, what keeps you
enemies when you are kin?

3
They fly above the same fields,
frighten the same farmers, carry the same seeds.

But the raven's tail will stiffen.
The crow will ruffle wings.

No matter how they pluck,
their feathers will not smooth.

4
The raven goes to the conference podium
and speaks of 20th century modernism.

The crow gives her own talk with slides
about 18th century Buddhism.

They circle each other during cocktails
and compare their beaks.

5
Don't they remember their shared childhood:
The thin-shelled egg, the poverty of straw?

The time will come when they'll shed their skin
and become gray shadows,

the color of the day ending,
the color of night coming on.

Father

The father has lived so long,
his skin is stretched translucent.
On/off buttons and blinking lights
shine through his paper lantern.

Each vein, a river
through parched valleys.
On each vein, a raft,
on each raft a story.

The father has reached a place
where none of us can follow.
He is smiling at something
none of us can see or hear.

He sits in a plaid armchair,
facing the streetside window,
the flutter of his nostrils
the only sign he's breathing.

Religion

At the fulcrum of the V-shaped roof,
silhouetted by morning,
a blackbird flapped nervously and took flight.

Chapel bells rang their funeral songs.
Skies gathered blue then gold then black.
Onlookers lined the dirt road like boarded-up buildings.

Lines of people kicked dust up the forgotten hill.
They hoisted the unvarnished box on
shoulders already sore from such tasks.

Up the steep slope, they trudged through sage and stone,
not out of love but duty did they go
under the sun's scorching stare.

Reverend Crumly was not loved, not even liked,
but nonetheless they shuffled forward.
A larger purpose pushed them on.

Reaching the precipice at the edge of town,
someone cried, *Shit in a bucket.*
At that signal, they heaved the pine box off the cliff.

Let the vultures have him now, a woman shouted.
He raped me, said one, "*He left me pregnant*, said another.
The children lifted shirts, showed the bruises of holy beatings.

Let us pray, a man said.
They gathered into a circle,
bowed their heads and thanked their God.

Subjunctive

If I told you the truth, I would cross the border without papers.
If you told me your secret, it would bend my back.
If we lose control of our past, the horizons will close in.
If I distract you from the bear, you will take the wrong trail.
If you draw my attention to the funnel cloud, I will jump down the well.
If we lose sight of the future, our compass will be useless.
If our lives have no heart, this poem will be hypothetical.
If this poem had no head, it would merely be confessional.
If the river had no mouth, words would flood the banks.
If the banks had no tellers, who could tell us what we're worth?

Fine Line

Looking back over your left shoulder,
you stand in the doorway, afraid of what's next.

The after-dinner light, jagged and scarlet
is tearing through the curtains.

The parquet is buckling
in the wake of a larger boat.

The fluorescent flickers on and off.
The split pea soup has frozen solid.

The clock stops ticking,
coughs and starts up again.

Our drying bodies dissolve into sand,
reassemble into castles on a new beach.

Is this a trick of the suggestible mind
or of the obstinate world?

Gifted

Once, when I left the piano room,
a sweater was tossed on the rocker,
a kettle murmured on the stove,
flowers turned to the window.

Even when I was alone,
she was in every song.
I couldn't talk in words,
but her hands were in every chord.

Now only the piano
inhabits the house.
I sleep all day with a chilly quilt
and play my scales every night.

Music hangs from a shelf, icicles from an eave.
The days are shorter, fewer now.
My frozen fingers fall hard on the keys.
Nails in a bucket.

Once, when I left the piano room,
a sweater was tossed on the rocker,
a kettle murmured on the stove,
flowers turned to the window.

Courtroom Drama

One day the judge no longer judged.
He no longer searched for guilt.
He no longer turned down his thumb
but threw up both his hands.

His gavel hammered not a nail.
His tweezers picked out shrapnel.
Bailiffs removed the handcuffs
and applied bandages instead.

He banished the expert witnesses,
turned to the court jester for advice.
He ordered the baffled lawyers
to put their motions into rhymes.

He ordered swords changed into flowers
and firearms into fireworks.
He let the orphans choose their mothers
and demanded everyone divorce.

Those in solitary confinement
and those twelve impartial jurors
were invited to a bacchanalia
by that nonjudgmental judge.

Free Will

I'm a ventriloquist's dummy.
Other people speak through my wooden jaws.

Where do those sounds come from?
Not from the oaken brain in my skull.

How I wish I were alone,
to put myself in the box at night.

to choose not the expected
but the surprise.

How can I bring words
up from my own cellar?

The coal comes in,
tumbling down the chute.

A furnace burns in the basement,
an uneasy thought for someone made of wood.

Out come the words,
still warm to the touch.

The Arrangement

I am sorry I neglected you, so sorry,
I was in my ermine fantasy,
sleepwalking
in my crystalline stiletto shoes
through aquarium hallways.

But there you were,
hair matted with rain,
nose against my window,
breath fogging the pane,
waiting like a cat to come in.

I should have been paying attention,
but I got distracted
by the electrodes on my fingers,
the turquoise beetles underfoot,
the telephone whining like a bee.

But I see you now.
Come in, come in.
Bow your head so I can dry your hair.
Lift your chin so our eyes can lock again.
Please accept my apology and eat this stone-cold soup.

Ghosts

Driving up the coastal highway,
lapping tides coming closer,
sliding across the flattened land
I passed the yellow bungalow

where we first undressed
for each other,
where we last traded
barbed words.

I turned away from the shoreline
and climbed into the mountains,
my foot pressed hard against the floor
to beat the predicted snowstorm.

The Searchers

I'm sure we'll find a restaurant soon.
It's been four hours and all we've seen
are boarded-up stores and browning fields.
The blacktop's yellow dashes pulsing by.

Rusted wrecks and dry arroyos.
A black vulture above our old Chevy wagon.
Let him spin himself dizzy; we're not turning back.
There's light behind the mountain and water too.

We come over a rise and there it is:
sun-catching chrome and neon letters, E-A-T.
One slice of cherry pie, two forks.
Back on the road, still not satisfied.

We come to the crest of the Continental Divide.
We park and walk to the cliff's edge.
The salt sea is too far away to smell
but close enough to imagine.

New York, New York

It was the curve in the earth,
the tunnel under the river
and the crease in our ambition that led us
to this strangely tangled jungle
to the dream deferred.

Our shared sense of wonder
drew us ever onward, into traps and out again,
between high rises and theaters,
within a cacophony of sirens and desires,
no difference between day and night.

An egg could fry on the sidewalk.
A man could freeze in the fairytale snow.
A saxophone could play the note between the piano keys.
A poet could cry from the fire escape –
Passers-by applauded, climbed the ladder.

The words and dances kept coming:
Animal cries, mathematical formulas,
angelic prayers, demonic curses, whirling our
childhood memories, after-death visions,
until, finished and forgotten, we could go home.

Page One

How do we start a book?
We know how it ends, but not how it starts.

We have a dictionary full of words.
We have stories we never told our children.

Couplets are scribbled on napkins from Pete's Bar.
A cardboard box of papers we wrote in college.

There's a ribbon around old letters
that no one unties anymore.

We have memories that have
changed from the actual events.

We have a kitchen drawer full of
rubber bands, toothpicks and stray screws.

In the refrigerator is leftover turkey, carrots and grapes,
no lettuce or potatoes.

How do we start a meal?
How do we start a journey?

We never used to ask for help,
but here we are asking now.

Everything we knew is gone.
All our best friends have passed on.

We want to top everything
we did before.

About the Authors

Geoffrey Himes' poetry has been published by Best American Poetry, December, Gianthology, Innisfree, Salt Lick and other publications. He has written about popular music and theater for the Washington Post, New York Times, Rolling Stone and many more since 1977. His book on Emmylou Harris, *In-Law Country*, was published in 2024 and his book of collaborative poems with Grace Cavalieri, *Fables from Italy and Beyond*, in 2025.

Grace Cavalieri was Maryland's tenth Poet Laureate (2018-2024). She founded and still produces "The Poet and the Poem" for public radio and podcasts, from the Library of Congress, celebrating 48 years on-air in 2025. She's an Academy of American Poets Fellow, with more than 30 books and chapbooks, and 20 plays produced on American stages. In July 2023, twenty-five years of her podcasts were sent to the moon from NASA on the Lunar Codex. Her recent book, *Owning the Not So Distant World*, was published by Blue Light Press.

www.ingramcontent.com/pod-product-compliance
Lightning Source LLC
Chambersburg PA
CBHW031219090426
42736CB00009B/980